STARFISH

STARFISH

By *Edith Thacher Hurd* • *Illustrated by Lucienne Bloch*

THOMAS Y. CROWELL COMPANY • *NEW YORK*

LET'S-READ-AND-FIND-OUT SCIENCE BOOKS

Editors: *DR. ROMA GANS,* Professor Emeritus of Childhood Education, Teachers College, Columbia University

DR. FRANKLYN M. BRANLEY, Chairman of The American Museum—Hayden Planetarium, consultant on science in elementary education

*AVAILABLE IN SPANISH

3   4   5   6   7   8   9   10

STARFISH

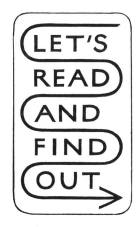
LET'S READ AND FIND OUT

Starfish live in the sea.

Starfish live deep down in the sea.

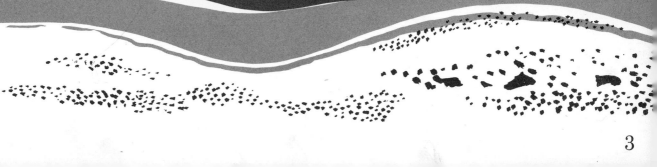

Starfish live in pools by the sea.

Some starfish are purple.

6

Some starfish are pink.

The mud star hides in the mud.

The brittle stars hide under rocks
in pools by the sea.
They are the tiniest starfish of all.

9

This is the sunflower starfish.
It is the biggest of all.

Starfish have many arms.
The arms are called rays.
Starfish have arms, but no legs.

Starfish have feet, but no toes.

They glide and slide
  on tiny tube feet.
They move as slowly as a snail.

A starfish has no eyes.

A starfish has no ears or nose.

His tiny mouth is on his underside.

When a starfish is hungry,
　he slides and he glides
　on his tiny tube feet.
He hunts for mussels and oysters
　and clams.

He feels for the mussels.
He feels for the oysters.
He feels for the clams.
He feels with his rays.
He feels for something to eat.

The starfish humps over a clam.

His rays go over it.

His rays go under it.

His rays go all over the clam.

The starfish pulls.

He humps and humps.

He pulls and pulls.

He pulls the shells open.

He eats the clam inside.

Sometimes a starfish loses a ray.
A crab may pull it off.
A rock may fall on it.
But this does not hurt.
It does not bother the starfish.
He just grows another ray.

In the spring when the sun shines warm,
　and the sea grows warm,
　starfish lay eggs.
Starfish lay eggs in the sand.
They lay many, many, many tiny eggs.
The eggs look like sand
　in the sea.

The tiny eggs float in the water.
They float up and down.
They move with the waves and the tide,
   up and down,
   up and down.

The tiny eggs grow into tiny starfish.
They float in the water.
They move with the waves,
   back and forth,
   back and forth.

The tiny starfish grow scratchy and hard.
They grow little rays.
They grow tiny tube feet
    to crawl on.

Baby starfish eat and eat
and EAT.

First they eat tiny things
   that float in the sea.
Then they eat mussels and oysters and clams.
They eat and they eat.
They grow and they grow.

There are many different starfish.
Some are fat.
Some are thin.
Some are prickly.
Some are prickly and pink.
Some are prickly and gray.
Some are just a tangle.

The basket starfish is a tangle,
  with rays that go up
  and rays that go down.
The rays of the big basket starfish
  go around
  and around.

Look on the rocks
by the sea.

Look in the pools
by the sea.

Look for starfish,
    the stars
        of the sea . . . .

ABOUT THE AUTHOR

EDITH THACHER HURD conducted the research for *Starfish* during an intensive period of study with her husband at the Marine Biology Laboratory in Portland, Oregon. Mr. and Mrs. Hurd examined the history and habits of "starfish and crabs, and things that live on the rocks."

Mrs. Hurd received her A.B. degree from Radcliffe College and continued her studies at the Bank Street College of Education in New York. During World War II, she worked for the Office of War Information in San Francisco.

Mrs. Hurd describes herself as "a Missourian by birth, a New Englander by education, a New Yorker by marriage, and now a happy Californian."

ABOUT THE ILLUSTRATOR

LUCIENNE BLOCH was born in Geneva, Switzerland. She received her early education in the United States and then returned to Europe to study art in Paris, Berlin, and Florence. She was among the first to work on designs for glass sculpture with the Leerdam Glass Works in Holland. With her husband, Stephen P. Dimitroff, she has painted murals in New York City, Michigan, and California.

Her work is also her hobby, and she has worked with many mediums. The unusual variety in her work has included ecclesiastical mosaics, portrait painting, and lectures to clubs and art organizations on topics related to many phases of art. Miss Bloch has received numerous awards for her achievements in ceramics, sculpture, printmaking, and book illustration.

Miss Bloch has lived in New York City; Cleveland, Ohio; and Flint, Michigan. The Dimitroffs and their three children make their home in Mill Valley, California.